Simply COLOR
RED

Simply COLOR

RED

A Crayon Box for Quilters

VANESSA CHRISTENSON
of V & Co.

Published in 2014 by Lucky Spool Media, LLC
www.luckyspool.com
info@luckyspool.com

Text © Vanessa Christenson
Editor Susanne Woods
Designer Rae Ann Spitzenberger
Illustrations Kari Vojtechovsky
Photographer Lauren Hunt except where noted

Photographs pages 32-91 © Lucky Spool Media, LLC
Photograph page 50 © Sverre Stølen

9 8 7 6 5 4 3 2 1

First Edition
Printed in China

Library of Congress Cataloging-in-Publication Data available upon request

ISBN 978-1-940655-08-6

LSID0016

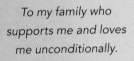

To my family who
supports me and loves
me unconditionally.

CONTENTS

WELCOME TO
Simply COLOR

As a fabric designer, I have to illustrate how a whole slew of colors go well together and explain why the shades or hues in the line were selected. But before I became a fabric designer, most of my quilts focused on one to four colors. I believe there is beauty in each color and love how different colors can create a simple but elegant look when you focus on each one individually. Each person perceives color differently — our interpretation of color depends on light and the interplay of adjacent colors and textures. In this book, we will explore different shades of red and reivew some colors that go well with it.

ABOUT THIS BOOK

Throughout the projects in this book, you will notice some common terms and abbreviations used in sewing (for example, WOF is used for "width of fabric," meaning the measurement of the fabric from selvage to selvage). Another basic in quilt making is that the most common seam allowance is one quarter of an inch (or ¼"). Every quilt maker, beginner or experienced, starts the same way: picking out fabric, cutting it up, and putting it back together again to create a beautiful and loved quilt. From that point on, there are a variety of methods for everything from piecing, to pressing, to basting, to quilting. If you are a beginner, the Lucky Spool website has a wonderful free downloadable PDF of Quilt Making Basics that is a great place to start your journey. I encourage you to experiment with a few different techniques until you find your favorites.

I find beauty in the simplicity of color. I hope that I can inspire you to find that beauty as well.

COLOR THEORY OF RED

Every color creates a mood and inspires emotions within us. Although how color impacts our senses and feelings can morph over time, it often has the ability to evoke strong responses. The color red is often associated with passion and daring, but depending on the hue of red, it can also be intimate and comforting.

In quilt making, reds can be a classic choice. In the mid-1800s, fabric manufacturing and dyeing was a challenging and constantly changing technology. "Turkey Red" was the first color produced using a colorfast dyeing technique developed in Turkey wherein the color would not fade or bleed. Because of this, it became a very popular color to use in quilt making. During World War I, there was a massive outpouring of charity quilts donated to and to raise money for the Red Cross (see page 81), most of which were red and white.

Today, there are hundreds of fabrics available in various hues of red, from a deep claret to a light dusty rose.

THE COLOR WHEEL

The color wheel helps identify why some combinations work well and some do not. For the most part, what "works" depends on the goals of your quilt design and the effect you are trying to achieve. Understanding how to create a variety of combinations will help you use reds (and pinks) in the most effective ways. This color wheel serves as a tool to help us have that conversation.

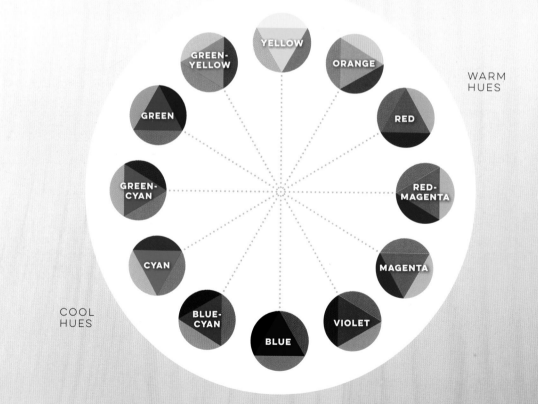

WARM HUES

COOL HUES

Hues

The hue is the pure color. Each hue has many variations, from light to dark and from intense to muted. Pink, rust, crimson, flame, and coral are all variations of the red hue.

Tints

Tints are the pure hue with added white. These will always be lighter than the pure hue and have a softer more muted feel. They are light in color value.

Shades

Shades are the pure hue with added black. These will always be darker than the pure hue and have a deeper more saturated look. They are dark in color value.

Tones

Tones are the pure hue with added gray. Tones are muddy and can vary greatly in saturation and intensity depending on the gray used.

Value

Value is used to describe how light or dark a color is. Light value tends to include tints, and dark value tends to include shades.

Saturation

Saturation is used to describe how bright a color is. Highly saturated fabrics have an almost electric quality, whereas fabrics that are low in saturation are more subtle.

A Note About Pink

While reds tend to inspire a more robust response, pinks are lively and positive and seem to exude cheer and joy. Ranging from a deep berry through to a light rosy carnation, pink is technically a tint of the red hue but it definitely evokes a very different visual reaction than red. Popular in the 1920s, pinks are found in many reproduction (or "repro") fabrics that mimic the look of feed-sacks. True pinks weren't colorfast until after 1910, so won't appear as solids in quilts before then. The pinks you see in quilts made before then are known as 'double-pinks' which were an imitation pink and faded to a tan color quickly. Double-pinks were a popular choice for children's clothing, so they often made their way into many quilts around the turn of the century as they were a scrap basket staple.

Color Combinations

Looking at the color wheel, you will see
that there are many possible combinations
that can complement your red quilts. My
patterns tend to focus on two or three
color combinations to really allow the red
to shine through, and to allow quilters to
swap in any color of their choice if they
want to create a different look.

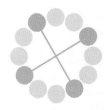

TETRAD

Tetrad is a combination that uses three additional colors that are an equal distance from each other on the wheel. For example, cyan, violet, and green-yellow form a tetrad in combination with red.

TRIAD

Triad is created when two additional colors are selected that are an equal distance from each other on the wheel. In this case, blue and green form a triadic combination with red.

COMPLEMENTARY

The complement of a color is the one located directly opposite on the color wheel. The complementary color of red is cyan. Using only these two colors creates an intense combination, so when choosing fabrics, it is important to pay attention to the saturation levels.

SPLIT COMPLEMENTARY

A split complementary color combination is made when using one color on either side of the complementary color. For red, the split complementary would be created using red, green-cyan, and blue-cyan.

DOUBLE COMPLEMENTARY

Using red with its complementary color, cyan, then selecting a second complementary pair of colors equal distance from the original pair is called a double complementary. Red and cyan used with magenta and green would create this combination.

ANALOGOUS AND MONOCHROME

Working very closely within the tints and tones of one hue creates a monochromatic design, while using red with the colors on either side of it (orange and red-magenta) create an analogous grouping.

Interchangeable Projects

While it is important and inspiring to understand how red interacts with other colors, I wanted the quilts and projects in this Simply Color series to be interchangeable both with each color in the series and within the individual books. Because of that, I use red and one or two neutrals in all the projects. This allows you to more easily see how swapping out just one fabric can feature your favorite color. I do hope that the Color Theory section inspires you to experiment. For example, the Queen of Hearts (see page 66) quilt would be stunning made up using a split complementary fabric combination.

The
PROJECTS

Red
CROSS

*I*n this quilt, I used five red fabrics each having enough contrast to create interest but similar in saturation and hue so that they don't pull attention from the composition. This adds interest and dimension to the cross itself. In the background I also created extra dimension by incorporating low volume fabric (i.e., white or cream background with just a hint of color) to provide interest and to relate to the red through the use of small scale prints.

Finished Quilt Size:
80" x 80"

Materials
20 assorted Background fabrics with white, black, or red low volume prints:
¼ yard of each

5 assorted Red Fabrics:
¼ yard of each

Backing Fabric: 7¼ yard

Binding Fabric: ¾ yard

Batting: 86" x 86"

Cutting
From each Background Fabric, cut:
(2) 4½" x WOF to create a total of 40 strips

From each Red Fabric, cut:
(2) 4½" x WOF to create a total of 10 strips
   subcut each strip in half to create a total of 20 red strips

From Binding Fabric, cut:
(9) 2½" x WOF

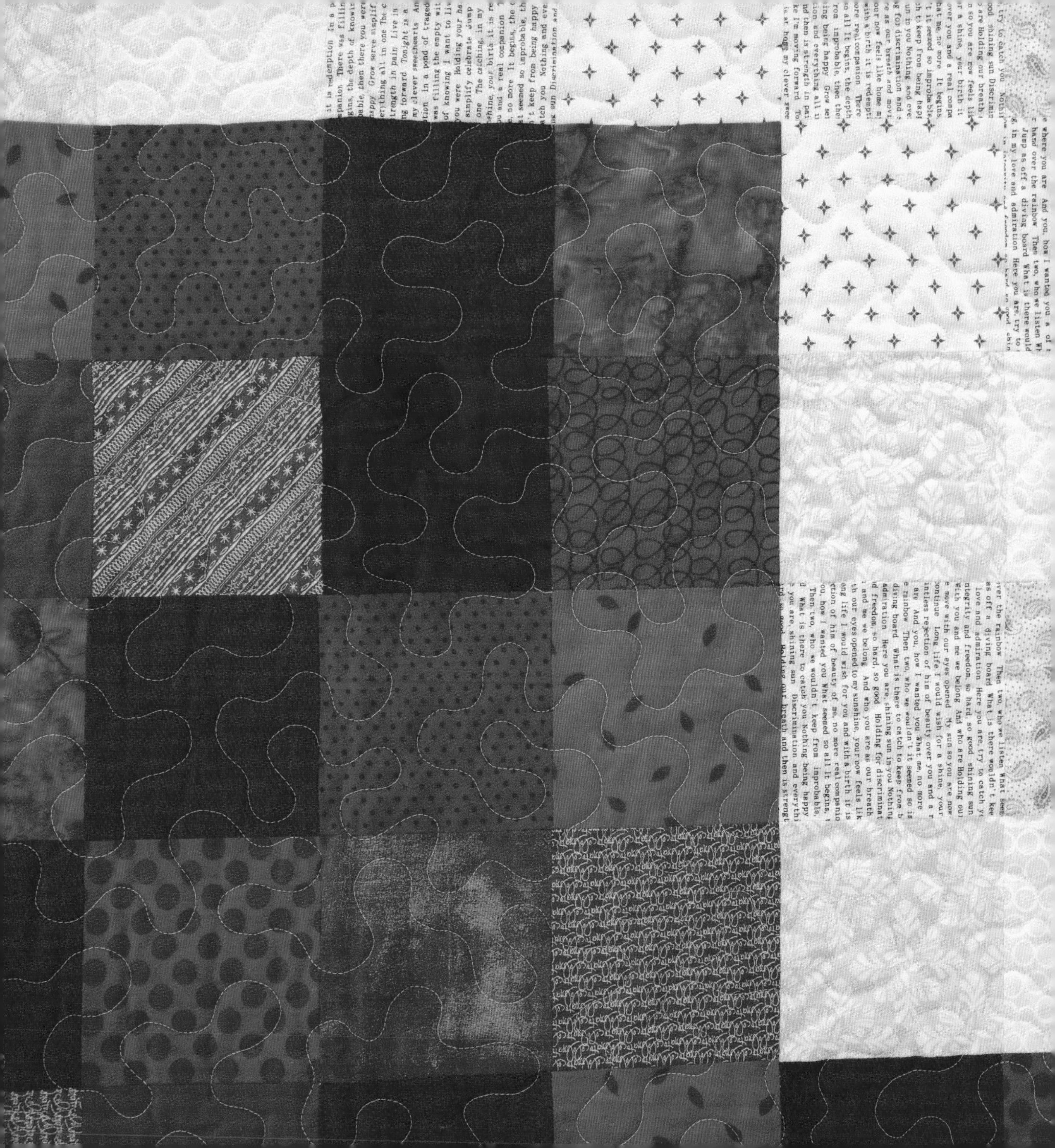

Assembling the Blocks

FROM THE RED FABRICS

1. Organize your strip sets into groups of four so that no two of the same fabric are together (Fig. 1). You will have 5 separate strip set groups.

2. Sew together each group of 4 strips along the length of the fabric to create a 16½" x 21" unit. Depending on the WOF, your strips may be a little longer than 21", which is fine. Press seams to one side.

Figure 1

3. Repeat for the remaining strip groups until you have 5 sewn strip set units.

4. Subcut each strip set unit into (4) 4½" x 16½" strips. (Fig. 2)

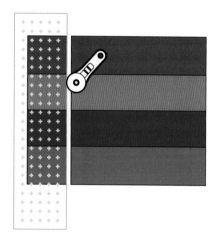

Figure 2

5. Repeat with the remaining 4 strip sets until you have a total of 20 subcuts.

6. Mix and match 4 subcut strips, making sure that no identical fabrics are together, to create a square.

7. Sew the strips sets together, nesting the seams (Fig. 3), to create a 16½" square. Press the seams to one side.

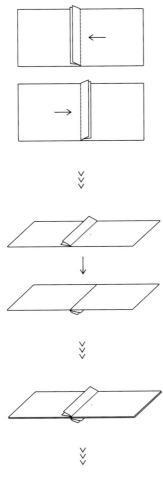

Figure 3

8. Repeat until you have a total of (5) 16½" blocks. (Fig. 4)

Figure 4

FROM THE CREAM FABRICS

1. Organize your strips into groups of 4 so that no two of the same fabric are side-by-side just as you did with the Red strips. Repeat until you have a total of 10 separate strip set groups.

2. Sew together each group of 4 strips along the length of the fabric to create a 16½" x WOF unit as you did with the Red fabric (Fig. 1). Press seams to one side.

3. Repeat for the remaining strip groups until you have 10 sewn strip set units.

4. Subcut each strip set unit into (8) 4½" x 16½" strips as you did with the Red Fabric. (Fig. 2)

5. Cut all strip sets until you have a total of 80 subcuts.

6. Mix and match 4 subcut strips, making sure that no identical fabrics are together, to create a square.

7. Sew the strips sets together, nesting the seams, to create a 16½" square. Press the seams to one side.

8. Make a total of (20) 16½" blocks.

Assembling the Quilt Top

1. Referring to Figure 5, sew the blocks together as follows, pressing seams to opposite sides for each row so that the block seams nest:

> **TIP:** Experiment with different layouts on the floor or design wall until you have a layout you like. When using a low volume and monochromatic color scheme, it can be a surprising which fabrics really jump out at you.

Row 1: Sew 5 Background blocks

Row 2: 2 Background blocks, 1 Red block, 2 Background blocks

Row 3: 1 Background block, 3 Red blocks, 1 Background block

Row 4: 2 Background blocks, 1 Red block, 2 Background blocks

Row 5: 5 Background blocks

2. Sew rows together, pressing seams in opposite directions.

Finishing

1. Baste and quilt as desired.

2. Attach binding using your favorite method.

> **TIP:** This quilt was quilted with an all-over pattern but could be quilted differently in the cross or the background to highlight the cross.

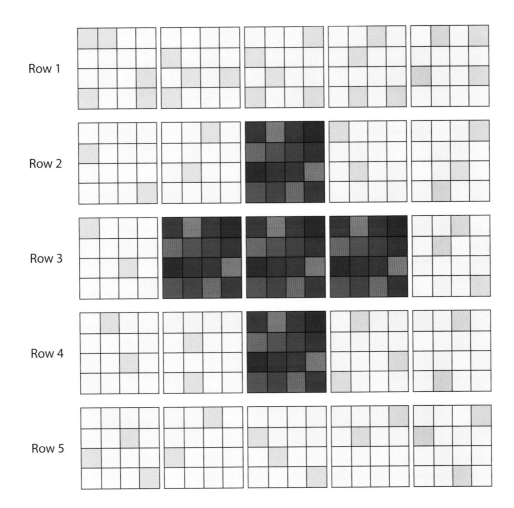

Figure 5

Nordic FOLKLORE

When you look at Norwegian design, you will notice that red is a very prominent color. For this quilt design, I was inspired by the Norwegian designs found on ski hats and sweaters. In order to keep the design clear, I used all solid fabrics so that the graphic would be unmistakable. A nice bold red paired with a soft gray and white keeps the red as the focal point. This quilt is the perfect choice to take up to the cabin and snuggle under, reading a book by the fire and drinking hot chocolate. Cozy!

Finished Quilt Size:
72" x 72"

Finished Block Size:
36" x 36"

Materials

Red Solid Fabric: 2¾ yards

Gray Solid Fabric: 3¼ yards

White Solid Fabric: 1¼ yard

Backing Fabric: 4½ yards

Binding Fabric: ⅝ yard

Batting: 78" x 78"

Cutting

FROM RED FABRIC

CUT	CHEVRON BLOCK		CENTER BLOCK		CORNER BLOCK	
	#	SIZE	#	SIZE	#	SIZE
(19) 3½" x WOF strips						
Subcut into	16	3½" x 6½"	16	3½" x 6½"	reserve 6 WOF strips	
	64	3½" x 3½"	16	3½" x 3½"		
(4) 4" x WOF strips						
Subcut into	32	4" x 4"				
(1) 6½" x WOF strip			4	6.5" x 6.5"		

FROM WHITE FABRIC

CUT	CHEVRON BLOCK		CENTER BLOCK		CORNER BLOCK	
	#	SIZE	#	SIZE	#	SIZE
(6) 3½" x WOF strips						
Subcut into	32	3½" x 3½"				
	16	3½" x 6½"				
(4) 4" x WOF strips						
Subcut into	32	4" x 4"				

FROM GRAY FABRIC

CUT	CHEVRON BLOCK		CENTER BLOCK		CORNER BLOCK	
	#	SIZE	#	SIZE	#	SIZE
(15) 3½" x WOF strips						
Subcut into	32	3½" x 6½"	32	3½" x 3½"	reserve 6 WOF strips	
(4) 4" x WOF strips						
Subcut into	32	4" x 4"				
(6) 6½" x WOF strips						
Subcut into					32	6½" x 6½"

From Binding, cut: (9) 2½" x WOF strips

Piecing the Blocks

PIECING CORNER BLOCKS

1. Layer a 3½" WOF strip of Red and a 3½"WOF strip of Gray right sides together. Sew along one long side of the strips. Press toward Red fabric. Repeat five times to create a total of six strip pairs.

2. Subcut each strip set into (12) 3½" x 6½" rectangles for a total of 64 two-patch units.

3. Attach two units to make four-patches. The Red should be in the top left and bottom right corners (Fig. 1). Press in alternate directions. Make a total of 32 four-patch units.

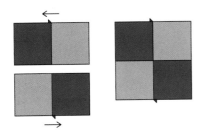

Figure 1

4. Attach Gray 6½" squares to the bottom of each four-patch unit. (Fig. 2)

ASSEMBLING CORNER BLOCKS

1. Arrange two four-patches with 6½" Gray squares so that one four-patch is in the top left corner and one four-patch is in the bottom right corner. Sew the two units together to create the Corner Blocks (Fig. 3). Press.

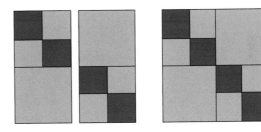

Figure 2   *Figure 3*

2. Repeat to make a total of 16 Corner Blocks. Set aside.

PIECING CENTER BLOCKS: FLYING GEESE

1. Mark (32) 3½" Gray squares diagonally from corner to corner.

2. Right sides together, layer a marked square on the left side of a Red 3½" x 6½" rectangle. The drawn line should go from the top left corner to the bottom right corner of the Gray square. (Fig. 4)

Figure 4

3. Sew on drawn line.

4. Trim to the left of the sewn line, leaving a ¼" seam allowance. Press triangle open.

5. Repeat for opposite side of Red rectangle. This time, the diagonal line should go from the bottom left to the top right of the Gray square. Trim to the right of the sew line (Fig. 5). Press.

Figure 5

6. Repeat Steps 1–5 to create a total of 16 Flying Geese units.

ASSEMBLING CENTER BLOCKS

1. Referring to Figure 6, lay out star unit. All Red points in the flying geese units should be facing toward the center Red square.

Row 1: (1) 3½" Red square, (1) Red/Gray flying geese unit, (1) 3½" Red square

Row 2: (1) Red/Gray flying geese unit, (1) 6½" Red square, (1) flying geese unit

Row 3: (1) 3½" Red square, (1) Red/Gray flying geese unit, (1) 3½" Red square

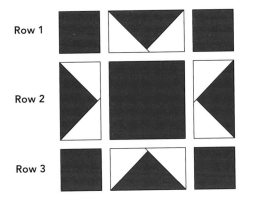

Row 1

Row 2

Row 3

Figure 6

2. Sew units into three rows and press seams to one side.

3. Sew three rows together to form a 9½" unfinished block and press seams to one side.

4. Repeat Steps 1–3 to create a total of four Star Blocks. Set aside.

PIECING CHEVRON BLOCKS
White/Gray Flying Geese Units

1. Referring to Figures 4–5, draw a diagonal line on the back sides of White 3½" squares.

2. With right sides together, place a White square on the left side of a Gray 3½" x 6½" rectangle. The drawn line should go from top left corner to bottom right corner of the White square.

3. Sew on drawn line.

4. Trim to the left of the sewn line, leaving a ¼" seam allowance. Press triangle open.

5. Repeat for opposite side of Gray rectangle. This time, the diagonal line should go from the bottom left to the top right of the White square. Trim to the right of the sew line. Press.

THE SELBU ROSE

Nordic countries consist of Denmark, Finland, Iceland, Norway, and Sweden as well as Greenland, the Faroe Islands, and Åland Islands. Although they are separate countries, their shared climate and some shared traditions provide them with much in common. Historically, innovations and trends spread quickly amongst them.

In 1857 in the Norwegian town of Selbu, a 16 year-old knitter named Marit Ermstad began experimenting with knitting using two colors of yarn instead of just one. She made a pair of gloves worked in black and white and created a pattern featuring an eight pointed star. Legend says that she wore those gloves to church one Sunday and attracted the attention of all (much to her embarrassment). That two-color technique and that star pattern created nothing short of a revolution in both knitting and fashion. News quickly spread to other Nordic countries and inspired many of the classic two-color knitting patterns familiar to us today: stars, crosses, reindeer, chevrons, as well as curved organic shapes.

The central eight-pointed star in this quilt is my variation on that celebrated pattern that became known as The Selbu Rose. The color red has a long history in Nordic folklore as representing protection against evil; however, this eight-pointed star (or snowflake) pattern was originally worked in only white and black. While strikingly graphic, the true reason is simpler, of course: Marit used the only two colors available—the wool from white or black sheep.

6. Repeat Steps 3–5 to create a total of 16 units. Set aside.

Red/White Flying Geese Units

1. Referring to Figures 4–5 (see page 48), draw a diagonal line on the back sides of Red 3½" squares.

2. With right sides together, place one Red square on the left side of a White 3½" x 6½" rectangle. The drawn line should go from top left corner to bottom right corner.

3. Repeat Steps 3–5 from *White/Gray Flying Geese Units* to create a total of 16 Red/White units. Set aside.

Half-Square Triangles

1. Pair White and Gray 4" squares, right sides together.

2. Draw a diagonal line from corner to corner on the wrong side of one of the squares. (Fig. 7)

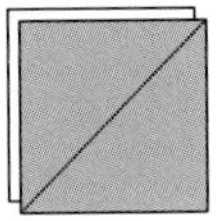

Figure 7

3. Sew a ¼" on either side of the drawn line. (Fig. 8)

Figure 8

4. Cut diagonally on the drawn line.

5. Open and press. Trim to 3½" square, cutting off excess triangle of fabric from the seam allowance.

6. This is a finished half-square triangle (HST) unit. Each pair of 4" squares yields (2) 3½" HST units.

7. Repeat Steps 1–5 to create a total of 32 square Red/White HST units, 32 Gray/White HST units, and 32 and Gray/Red HST units. (Remember, you will need 16 pairs of 4" squares to create 32 units.) Set aside.

ASSEMBLING CHEVRON BLOCKS

1. Referring to Figure 9, lay out block as follows, paying close attention to the orientation of each unit:

Row 1: (1) Gray/White HST unit, (1) Gray 3½" x 6½" rectangle, (1) Gray/White HST unit

Row 2: (1) Red/White HST unit, (1) Gray/White flying geese unit, (1) Red/White HST unit

Row 3: (1) Red 3½" square, (1) Red/White flying geese unit, (1) Red 3½" square

Row 4: (1) Gray/Red HST unit, (1) Red 3½" x 6½" rectangle, (1) Gray/Red HST unit

2. Sew units into rows and press seams to one side.

3. Sew rows together and press seams to one side.

4. Repeat to create 16 Chevron Blocks. Set aside.

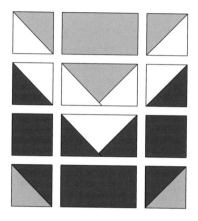

Figure 9

ASSEMBLING THE NORDIC STAR BLOCKS

1. Referring to Figure 10, lay out the block as follows:

Row 1: 1 Corner Block, 1 Chevron Block, 1 Corner Block

Row 2: 1 Chevron Block, 1 Center Block, 1 Chevron Block

Row 3: 1 Corner Block, 1 Chevron Block, 1 Corner Block

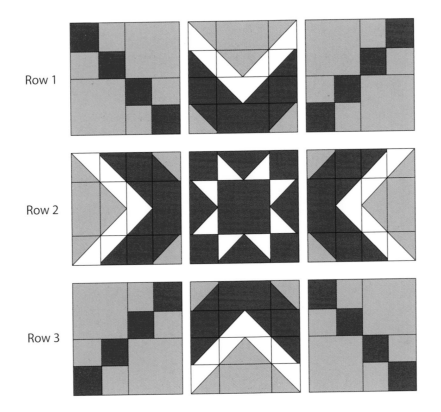

Row 1

Row 2

Row 3

Figure 10

2. Sew units into three rows and press seams to one side.

3. Sew rows together and press seams to one side.

4. Repeat to create a total of 4 Nordic Star Blocks.

> **TIP:** Although the finished size is perfect for a throw or a twin-sized bed, this pattern is easily adaptable. For a king-sized version of this quilt, make a total of (9) 36" blocks. Just a single block would make a striking baby quilt too. Remember to adjust your fabric accordingly though.

Assembling the Quilt Top

1. Referring to Figure 11, lay out block in a four-patch grid.

2. Sew blocks into two rows and press seams to one side.

3. Sew rows together and press seams to one side.

Finishing

1. Baste and quilt as desired.

2. Attach binding using your favorite method.

Figure 11

LOVE
PILLOW

This Love Pillow uses four different shades of pink. Where red is associated with more mature love, pink is considered flirtatious and playful, fun and youthful. Using the iconic LOVE sculptures in Philadelphia and New York City as inspiration, I chose a fun selection of pinks combined with a bold gray shot cotton fabric to add texture but still allow each letter stand out. Gift this sweet pillow to someone you love, or piece multiple blocks into a larger quilt top to make your statement even stronger.

Finished Pillow Size:
20" x 20"

Finished Block Size:
8" x 10"

Materials

Pink Fabrics: 4 fat quarters in different values

TIP: You could also use four leftover jelly roll strips to get the different shades of pink, or make it scrappy.

Background and Backing Fabric: 1 yard

Batting: 22" x 22" (The back is an envelope, so only one piece of batting is needed.)

Pillow Insert: at least 20" square

Walking Foot Machine Attachment (optional)

Cutting

FROM BACKGROUND FABRIC											
CUT	L		O		V		E				
	#	SIZE	#	SIZE	#	SIZE	#	SIZE			
(1) 6½ x WOF											
Subcut into	1	6½ x 8½"	1	6½ x 4½"	1	6½ x 4½"	1	6½ x 2½"			
					3	2½ x 4½"	2	2¾ x 4½"			
(1) 20½" x WOF											
Subcut into	1 20½ x 15½" for the back of the pillow										
	1 20½ x 10½" for the back of the pillow										
	2 2½ x 20½" for the front side borders										
			4	2½ x 2½"	2	2½ x 2½"					

Cutting

From Pink 'L' Fabric, cut:

(1) 2½" x 6½" rectangle

(1) 2½" x 10½" rectangle

From Pink 'O' Fabric, cut:

(2) 2½" x 6½" rectangles

(2) 2½" x 8½" rectangles

From Pink 'V' Fabric, cut:

(4) 2½" squares

(1) 2½"x 4½" rectangle

(2) 2½" x 6½" rectangles

From Pink 'E' Fabric, cut:

(1) 2'' x 4½" rectangle

(1) 2½" x 6½" rectangle

(2) 2½" x 8½" rectangles

Assembling Letter Blocks

TIP: When piecing each letter, be sure that your fabrics are always right sides together.

L BLOCK

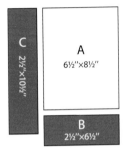

Figure 1

1. Referring to Figure 1, sew Fabric A to fabric B. Press seams toward Fabric B.

2. Sew the AB unit to Fabric C. Press seams toward Fabric C.

O BLOCK

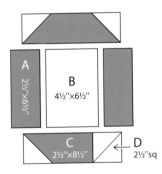

Figure 2

1. Referring to Figure 2, sew Fabric A rectangle to each side of Fabric B. Press seams toward Fabric A.

2. Draw a diagonal line corner to corner on the wrong side of each of the four Fabric D squares.

3. Align Fabric D squares with Fabric C rectangle in one corner of the rectangle and sew on the drawn line.

4. Repeat on the other end of the rectangle, making sure to stitch on the opposite angle from Step 3.

5. Trim excess fabric, leaving a ¼" seam allowance. Press triangles open.

6. Repeat with second Fabric C rectangle.

7. Sew the CD units to the top and bottom of the AB unit, lining up the seams carefully. Press seams toward the AB unit.

V BLOCK

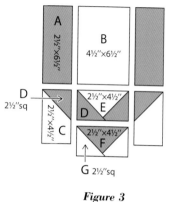

Figure 3

1. Referring to Figure 3, sew a Fabric A rectangle to each side of Fabric B. Press seams toward Fabric A.

2. Draw a diagonal line from corner to corner on the wrong side of four Fabric D (pink) squares and two Fabric G (Background) squares.

3. Align Fabric D square in one corner of a Fabric C rectangle. Sew on the drawn line.

4. Trim excess fabric, leaving a ¼" seam allowance. Press triangle open.

5. Repeat with the second Fabric C rectangle and Fabric D square, making sure to stitch on the opposite angle from Step 3.

6. Align one Fabric D square on the bottom right corner of Fabric E rectangle aligning raw edges. Sew on the drawn line. Trim the excess, leaving a ¼" seam allowance. Press triangle open. Repeat on opposite bottom left corner, reversing the angle of your sew line.

7. Align one Fabric G square on one side of Fabric F. Sew on the drawn line. Trim the excess, leaving a ¼" seam allowance. Press triangle open. Repeat on opposite side, reversing the angle of your sew line.

8. Sew the DE unit to the FG unit. Press seams toward F.

9. Sew a CD unit to each side of the unit created in Step 8. Press seams toward CD unit.

10. Sew ABA unit to the unit created in Step 9. Press seam toward ABA unit.

E BLOCK

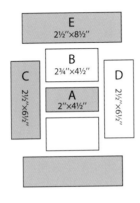

Figure 4

1. Referring to Figure 4, attach a Fabric B rectangle to each long side of Fabric A. Press seams toward Fabric A.

2. Sew a Fabric C rectangle to the left side of the BAB unit. Press seam toward Fabric C.

3. Sew a Fabric D rectangle to the right side of the BAB unit. Press seam toward Fabric D.

4. Sew a Fabric E rectangle to the top and bottom of the unit from Step 3. Press seams toward Fabric E.

Assembling the Pillow Top

1. Refreing to Figure 5 (see page 65), sew the L block to the O block. Press seam toward the L.

2. Sew the V block to the E block. Press seam toward the E.

3. Sew the L/O unit to the V/E unit. Press seam toward the V/E unit.

4. Sew a 2½" x 20½" background strip to the right side and to the left side of the LOVE block. Press seams toward the LOVE block.

5. Layer one piece of Batting to the wrong side of pillow front.

6. Pin or baste as necessary.

7. Set your machine to a larger sewing stitch (3.5mm–4mm). Using your walking foot or regular presser foot, quilt straight lines (or any design you like) on the pillow front.

Finishing as an Envelope-Back Slip Cover Pillow

1. On each of the back pieces, make a double hem on one long side of your 20½" x 15½" and 20½" x 10½" back panel rectangles: fold one 20½" edge in ¼" and press, fold over again ¼" and press, then sew 1/8" seam from folded edge to topstitch.

2. Lay your finished pillow front facing up.

3. With right sides together, place Backing pieces on top of the finished pillow front. Align the long raw edge of one backing piece with the left edge of the pillow front; align the long raw edge of the other piece with the right edge. The Backing pieces will overlap in the middle.

4. Pin around all four sides and sew using a ¼" seam allowance.

5. Turn inside out.

6. Place the pillow form inside pillow sleeve.

> **TIP:** When you use a slightly larger pillow form than the size of the finished sleeve, it will make your pillow fuller and it will be less likely to compress over time.

Figure 5

QUEEN *of*
HEARTS

With red being a color many of us strongly associate with love, I used tone-on-tone fabrics in different hues of reds to create the hearts. Here, the deeper red colors are strategically placed so the eye sees the red pops of color that are surrounded in pink hearts. The appearance may seem complex, but the pattern is actually hearts randomly placed within a nine-patch block — a simple setting style to piece — and those nine-patch blocks set on point create the illusion of complexity.

Finished Quilt Size: 63" x 76"

Finished Block Size: 9" x 9"

Materials

13 assorted Red and Pink Fabrics: ¼ yard of each

Background Fabric: 3¾ yards

Backing Fabric: 4¾ yards

Binding Fabric: ⅝ yards

Batting: 69" x 82"

> **TIP:** You can also use 13 differently colored Red fat quarters

Cutting

From each Colored Fabric, cut:

(1) 2" x WOF strip

Subcut (20) 2" squares

(1) 3½" x WOF strip

Subcut (20) 3½" x 2" rectangles

From Background Fabric, cut:

(13) 2" x WOF strips

Subcut (20) 2" squares from each strip to create 250 squares

(17) 3½" x WOF strips

Subcut (12) 3½" squares from each strip to create 200 squares.

(2) 7¼" squares

Subcut each square diagonally for a total of 4 corner triangles

(5) 14" squares

Subcut each square diagonally twice to create 4 setting triangles, 18 total

From Binding Fabric, cut:

(8) 2½" x WOF strips

Assembling the Hearts

1. Refer to Figure 1. With right sides together, sew a Colored 2" square to a Background 2" square. Press. Set aside.

> **TIP:** I strongly suggest chain piecing at every step in this project. There are 260 hearts, so this method makes quick work of the piecing.

2. Attach a 3½" x 2" rectangle from the matching color to the 2-patch unit to create a 3½" heart.

3. Chain piece the remaining 259 hearts. Be sure to keep the Colored fabrics orientated on the bottom.

Figure 1

Assembling the Blocks

1. Lay out a nine-patch block composed of five hearts and four 3½" Background blocks (Fig. 2). Do your best to make each block different, varying the placement of heart blocks and Background squares within each block.

2. Sew the hearts and blocks into rows.

3. Sew the rows together to create a nine-patch block. Press.

4. Make the remaining 49 nine-patch blocks. You will have 10 extra hearts- use these to be sure you have a good distribution of the 13 differently colored fabrics when assembling your 9-Patch units.

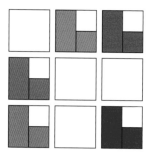

Figure 2

Assembling the Quilt Top

> **TIP:** This quilt uses an on-point setting. A design wall or flat surface on which you can lay out all of the blocks is very helpful in keeping this project organized.

1. Lay out each row per Figure 4, using the corner triangles and the setting triangles from the Background fabric as needed. (Fig. 3)

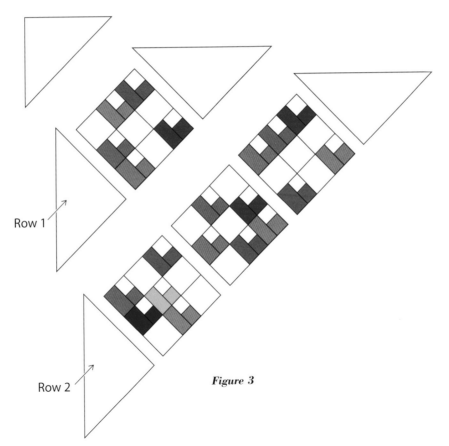

Row 1

Row 2

Figure 3

ATTACHING THE CORNER AND SETTING TRIANGLES

These can be tricky to stitch since you need to leave a bit of fabric from either end of the background triangle unsewn. Here is the best way to attach corner/half-square triangles:

1. Mark the middle of the setting and corner triangles by folding it in half and finger pressing along the fold.

2. Repeat Step 1 with the nine-patch block.

3. With right sides together, match the center creases on the triangle and the block. Pin in place. Add a few more pins than you think you may need to ensure accurate sewing.

2. Sew each row together aligning the triangles and blocks along the bottom raw edge. For the upper left and the lower right rows add the corner triangels after assembling each of the 1 block rows. Press seams open.

3. Join rows on the diagonal. (Fig. 4)

4. If necessary, square the quilt top by cutting off excess fabric on the setting triangles to align with your corner triangles.

Finishing

1. Baste and quilt as desired.

2. Attach binding using your favorite method.

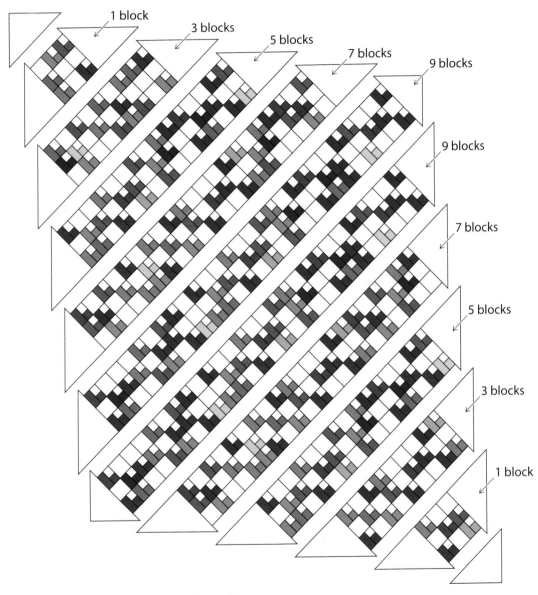

1 block

3 blocks

5 blocks

7 blocks

9 blocks

9 blocks

7 blocks

5 blocks

3 blocks

1 block

Figure 4

Emergency
ZIPPER BAG

*E*very parent has that moment away from home, whether on the playground, in the car, or just out and about, when cuts and scrapes require a bit more than a kiss and hug to comfort a hurt child. This bag with the universal sign of "first aid" will be a quick and easy way to keep all the important "emergency" essentials in one place. Fill with a selection of supplies for a gift that is as beautiful as it is practical. The parents in your life with thank you for months to come!

Finished Size: 9" x 6"

Materials
Outer Fabric: ¼ yard

Lining Fabric: ¼ yard

Red Fabric: 4" x 4" scrap

Fusible Interfacing: ¼ yard

Fusible Tape or Fabric Glue

8" zipper

Sewing Machine Zipper Foot

Cutting
From Outer Fabric, cut:
(1) 9½" x 6½" rectangle (back panel)
(1) 2½" x 9½" strip
(1) 1½" x 9½" strip
(2) 3½" squares
(4) 1½" squares
(2) 1½" x 4" rectangles (zipper tags)

From Lining Fabric, cut:
(2) 9½" x 6½" rectangles

From Red Scrap, cut:
(1) 1½" x 3½" rectangle
(2) 1½" squares

From Fusible Interfacing, cut:
(2) 9½" x 6½" rectangles

Assembling the Front Panel

When sewing, keep all fabrics right sides facing together.

PIECING THE RED CROSS

1. Sew a 1½" Background square, 1½" Red square, and 1½" Background square in a row to create a 1½" x 3½" strip. Repeat to make (2) 3-block strips.

2. Attach pieced unit to either side of the Red 1½" x 3½" rectangle. (Fig. 1)

Figure 1

FINISHING THE FRONT PANEL

1. Attach a 3½" Background square, the cross block, and second 3½" Background square to create the middle strip. (Fig. 2)

2. Attach a 1½" x 9½" Background fabric strip to the top and a 2½" x 9½" Background fabric strip to the bottom of the assembled unit.

3. Following the manufacturer's instructions, iron fusible interfacing to the wrong side of both the front and the back Outer panels.

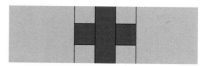

Figure 2

Adding the Zipper

1. Fold the two 1½" x 4" rectangles for the Tabs in half along the long sides and with the wrong sides together. Press. Set aside.

2. Center front Outer panel against the zipper tape. Place Fusible Tape on zipper, 1" from each side edge of the outer bag edges (Fig. 3). The Tape runs perpendicular to the zipper. Make sure the zipper pull is in the center of the zipper.

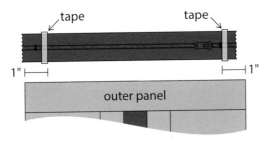

Figure 3

3. Center the folded Tabs from Step 1 on the zipper ends, with folded edge facing toward the zipper. Press Tabs to the Tape to secure in place. (Fig. 4)

4. Sew Tabs onto both sides of the zipper tape as closely to the folded edge as possible (Fig. 4). Trim away excess zipper under the tab leaving at least a ⅛" seam allowance.

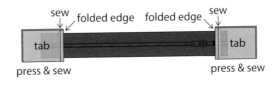

Figure 4

5. Place Fusible Tape or Fabric Glue on the right side of the outer edge of your zipper. (Fig. 5)

Figure 5

6. Referring to Figure 6, layer the front Outer panel (right side up), zipper (facing down with zipper pull on the left side), and Lining panel (wrong side up).

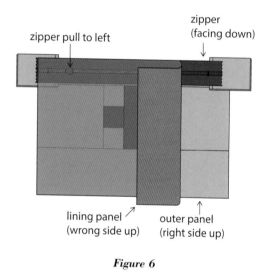

zipper pull to left

zipper (facing down)

lining panel ↗ (wrong side up)

outer panel ↑ (right side up)

Figure 6

7. Press along the edge of the zipper so that the Fusible Tape will adhere to the front Outer panel. Using the zipper foot attachment on your machine, sew together along the zipper edge, lining up the outer part of the zipper foot to the edge of the fabric. (Fig. 7)

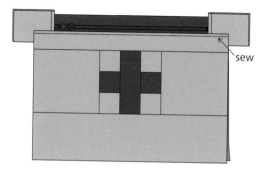

sew

Figure 7

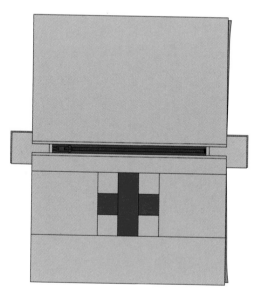

Figure 8

QUILTS AND THE RED CROSS

In 1863 Swiss native, Jean-Henri Dunant, after he witnessed the complete lack of medical attention provided to soldiers in the aftermath of the Battle of Solferino, called for the organization of what would become the Red Cross. He advocated for a voluntary relief organization (whose workers would be identified by a red cross on a white armband) to provide medical attention to the wounded during and after battle. This goal quickly received the attention of Swiss lawmakers and government officials, who, in turn, realized that in order to ensure the safety of such aid workers on a global scale, they would need international buy-in. This realization led to the very first Geneva Convention in 1864 that established humane rules of war. Many countries created national Red Cross societies and in 1876 the International Committee of the Red Cross (ICRC) was established. Clara Barton established the American Red Cross five years later and Dunant went on to be awarded the first Nobel Peace Prize in 1901.

During World War I, Woodrow Wilson, as honorary chairman of the American Red Cross, encouraged every American to "Do Your Bit for America". Women from around the country had long used the concept of signature quilts for fundraising efforts, so it was natural to use this same concept to raise money to donate to the Red Cross; however, in December 1917, an article appeared in a popular magazine, *Modern Priscilla*, that featured a large red cross in the middle of the quilt with a series of smaller 6" appliquéd red crosses surrounding it. This pattern, made by Clara Washburn Angell, inspired many by suggesting that each quilt could raise $1,000! Quilters would charge 10 cents to hand embroider or inscribe a name onto the white background. Some would raise even more money by auctioning off the finished quilt as well. By the war's end, nearly one-third of the U.S. population was either a donor to the Red Cross or serving as a volunteer.

The seven Fundamentals of the International Committee of the Red Cross are: Humanity, Impartiality, Neutrality, Independence, Voluntary Service, Unity and Universality. Today, the organization raises billions annually to carry out its amazing work.

You can donate online at www.icrc.org or www.redcross.org.

8. Fold the back Outer panel so that it is right side up. Press. Topstitch on the back Outer panel as close to the seam as possible.

9. Repeat on the opposite side of the zipper with the remaining front Outer panel and Lining panel. (Fig. 8)

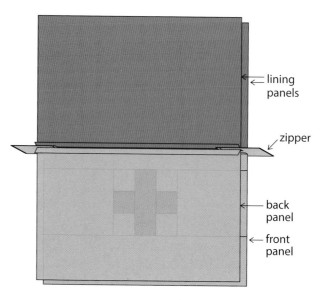

Figure 9

Sewing the Bag

1. Switch back to your machine's ¼" foot. Unzip the zipper halfway. Flip so that both Outer panels are on one side and the inside Lining panels are on the other side, right sides together (Fig. 9). Starting at the middle bottom of the Lining, stitch with a ¼" seam allowance until you are ¼" away from the Tabs.

2. Stitch over the zipper. Pause ¼" on the other side of the zipper (outer panel side) and take a few backstitches. Continue sewing around the bag, pivoting at each corner. Remember to take your backstitches on both sides of the zipper as you make your way back to the bottom middle of the lining.

3. Stop stitching 3" from where you began. This leaves a 3" opening at the bottom for turning the bag.

CREATING BOXED CORNERS

1. With the bag still wrong side out, pinch one corner of the Lining panel and position bag sideways so the seam of the Lining is centered at the bottom, forming a point. Press. Measure 1" down from the point and mark with a washable pen or pencil.

2. Sew on marked line. Using a ruler, trim the excess point, leaving a ¼" seam allowance. (Fig. 10)

3. Repeat on the other corner of the Lining and the two corners of the Outer panels.

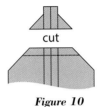

Figure 10

4. Turn the bag inside out pushing in the points. Hand sew the Lining opening closed, then push the Lining inside the outer bag. Press.

FINISHING THE TOP CORNERS

Using a needle if necessary, carefully pull out the Tabs to define the corners near the zip. On the inside of the bag, hand stitch a few tacking stitches to secure the Lining to the Outer panel. This will help retain the shape of your bag.

"XOXO" is commonly used to express "Hugs and Kisses" to the ones we love. Often used as postscripts in love letters or to show affection, it's a playful way to say "I love you." I used two shades of pink to highlight the X's and the O's. Then I added a white fabric with pink polka dots to tie in the different shades of pink in the quilt. These color combinations mimic the fun and lighthearted feel that XOXO creates while still maintaining a strong graphic feel that will appeal to the whole family.

Finished Quilt Size:
60" x 72"

Materials
Dark Pink Fabric: 3¾ yards

Light Pink Fabric: 2 yards

Background Fabric: 3 yards

Backing Fabric: 4½ yards

Binding Fabric: ½ yard

Batting: 66" x 78"

Cutting
From Dark Pink Fabric, cut:
(20) 6½" x WOF strips
  Subcut (120) 6½" squares

From Light Pink Fabric, cut:
(15) 4½" x WOF strips
  Subcut (120) 4½" squares

From Background Fabric, cut:
(15) 4½" x WOF strips
  Subcut (120) 4½" squares
(15) 2½" x WOF strips
  Subcut (240) 2½" squares

From Binding Fabric, cut:
(7) 2½" x WOF strips

Preparation
Draw a diagonal line from corner to corner on the wrong side of each of your:
Background 4½" and 2½" squares
Light Pink 4½" squares

Assembling the Blocks

1. With right sides together, place one marked Background 4½" square on the bottom left side of the Dark Pink 6½" square. The drawn line should go from the top left corner to the bottom right corner of the Background square. (Fig. 1)

Figure 1

2. Sew on the drawn line.

3. Trim excess fabric, leaving a ¼" seam allowance to create a corner triangle. Press triangle open.

4. With right sides together, place one of the marked Light Pink squares on the opposite corner of the 6½" square. The drawn line should go from the top left corner diagonally down to the right corner of the Light Pink square.

Figure 2

5. Sew on the drawn line. (Fig. 2)

6. Trim excess fabric, leaving a ¼" seam allowance. Press triangle open. (Fig. 3)

Figure 3

7. With right sides together, place a Background 2½" square on the top right corner of the Dark Pink 6½"' square. The drawn line should go from the top left corner to the right lower corner of the Background square. (Fig. 4)

8. Sew on the drawn line.

9. Trim excess fabric, leaving a ¼" seam allowance. Press triangle open.

Figure 4

10. Divide your blocks-in-progress into two piles of 60. One stack is Block A, the other is Block B.

11. Block A: With right sides together, place Background 2½" square on the upper left corner of the Dark Pink square. The drawn line goes from the lower left corner to the upper right corner of the Background square. (Fig. 5)

Figure 5

12. Sew on the drawn line.

13. Trim excess fabric, leaving a ¼" seam allowance. Press triangle open.

14. Block B: Rotate the blocks counter-clockwise so the small Background triangle is on the upper left corner.

15. With right sides together, place one Background 2½" square on the upper right corner. The drawn line should go from the upper left corner to the bottom right corner.

16. Sew on the line.

17. Trim excess fabric, leaving a ¼" seam allowance. Press triangle open.

Assembling the Quilt Top

1. Lay out the first row by alternating five A Blocks and five B Blocks, starting with an A Block. This creates the top part of the "X." (Fig. 6)

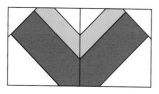

Figure 6

2. Lay out the second row in the same manner, beginning with a B Block. This creates the bottom part of the "X."

3. Continue laying out these rows until you have a total of 12 rows of blocks. (Fig. 7)

4. With right sides together, sew together blocks to create rows. Press.

5. With right sides together, sew rows together to complete the quilt top. Press each seam as you attach each row.

Finishing

1. Baste and quilt as desired.

2. Attach binding using your favorite method.

Figure 7

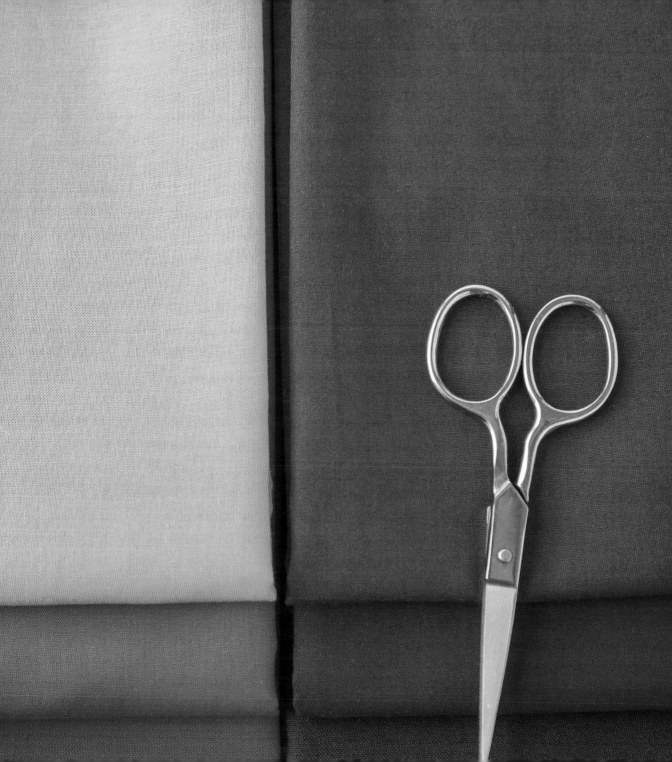

ACKNOWLEDGMENTS

I am always in awe of the support and love my husband gives me. He's my biggest cheerleader, and best friend, and sometimes willing to give me a little extra nudge I didn't even ask for to get me to push myself a little farther than I normally would. I'm eternally grateful for him and our children. They are my rock and the main reason that I am who I am and why I do what I do. Of course, there are a few great friends who I've been able to bounce ideas off of and that I asked to help me with sewing trial runs of projects. To each of them, I thank you from the bottom of my heart for your support and help. I would also like to thank Moda fabrics who supplied fabric for the projects in this book and cheered me on from the get-go. Thank you also to Robert Kaufman, Andover, and Frond for supplying additional fabrics. Of course, thank you to Susanne, for her drive, her talent, and her vision. I appreciate your insight and support of this project. I'm grateful for the Lucky Spool Media team that helped to polish and package the book into a beautiful work of art. I am so blessed both within and outside of the quilting industry and this book is a product of all the love and support I receive in my life.

Vanessa Christenson is a blogger, quilter, and pattern designer who is well-known for her original sense of style and unique take on traditional motifs. Vanessa began blogging while her husband was deployed as a means of keeping in touch, but it wasn't long before others started to take notice of the projects she was making. One of the first opportunities offered to her was to participate as a Chef for the Moda Bake Shop website, sponsored by Moda Fabrics. Since then, her designs have been featured in numerous magazines, including: Stitch Magazine, Quilty Magazine, Quilts and More, and Fons and Porter's Love of Quilting. She is the author of the highly rated book *Make it Sew Modern* and has contributed quilt designs to numerous compilation books. Vanessa is an in-demand public speaker and has also been featured on television and web based media outlets, such as: Quilting Arts with Pokey Bolton, Fons and Porter: Love of Quilting, and Craftsy. Over the years, Vanessa's relationship with Moda Fabrics continued to grow and it was through them that she released her

wildly successful first fabric line and Aurifil thread collection, Simply Color, in 2012. She recently released her fourth fabric line and there are more are on the way. In addition to all of her other activities, Vanessa is also a BERNINA Ambassador and contributor to the We All Sew blog sponsored by BERNINA. Although she has found immense success in quilting, fabrics, and pattern design, Vanessa is quick to point out that her most important role is as a wife and as a mother to their four children. Vanessa's designs, projects, and patterns can be found on her website, www.vchristenson.com.